Get Up and Goal

A simple guide to setting and achieving goals

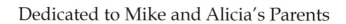

Dedicated to Mike and Alicia's Parents

PRESENTED TO

FROM

DATE

About the Author

Alicia Hadley is an author, public speaker, musician, graphic designer, entrepreneur and youth mentor. With over a decade of working with youth and young adults, Alicia understands the overwhelming challenges this generation faces. Her books, "My Simple Book of Goals" and "Get Up and Goal" help to encourage a conqueror's mentality and stimulate the drive to achieve success. As a speaker, Alicia engages her audience with humor and wisdom. Her interactive and thought-provoking approach captivates her listeners. Undoubtedly, Alicia's professional, yet "down-to-earth," personality renders an empowering message.

Alicia is a wife and mother. In her free time she loves bonding with her family and song writing. She is also the founder of Freecupcakewraps.com.

Her message to youth:

"Don't just sit there…Get up and Goal!"

Visit **www.GetupandGoal.com** to engage Alicia Hadley to speak at your event and to download printable "Goal Achievement Awards."

A Note on Humility

As you set and accomplish your goals, it is important to always remain humble. The online Urban Dictionary gives a great definition of this word. It states that being humble is:

> "An admirable quality that not many people possess. It means that a person may have accomplished a lot, or be a lot but doesn't feel it is necessary to advertise or brag about it."

I believe a humble person is also one who doesn't mind learning from others; accepting correction or instruction that may be helpful to them. A humble person will never boast that they are better than anyone else, nor purposely make others feel bad about not reaching the same goals that they have achieved. You won't find it necessary to always be the center of conversation or attention if you are humble. Instead, you show genuine interest and concern for others. You celebrate and congratulate others when they share good news and accomplish their goals.

Sometimes it's difficult to be humble especially if you're really good at something. However, admitting that you're not perfect and that there's room for improvement can help. The truth is, most people prefer not to be around those who brag and boast, and want attention all the time. So if you want success, lasting friendships and great opportunities, try a humble approach to setting and achieving your goals.

GET UP AND GOAL

A simple guide to setting and achieving goals

I LET HIM WIN!

Growing up, my dad would always challenge me to races. My mom wasn't too fond of them but that's probably because the races would often be in public places such as crowded malls and grocery store isles. Anyway, I remember times when we would walk outside of a mall and suddenly dad would say, "Hey, I'll race ya to the car." Of course, I always replied, "OK." And before I knew it he would yell, "Ready, set, go" and literally take off running while I was left standing there trying to find the starting line. Then there were those planned races to the mailbox; we would be playing outside and dad would say, "Let's race to the mailbox, here's the starting line." I'd reply, "Ok." We'd take our positions and he would yell, "Ready, set, go!" You guessed it, by the time I made it half way to the mailbox he was at the finish line.

Those races continued throughout my high school days. And although I loved racing him, I was always left wondering how my dad continued to beat me—I considered myself in great athletic shape.

I was a basketball player, participated in numerous school activities and was pretty healthy. My dad, on the other hand — well his serious athletic days were over so I considered him a sports veteran (lol…I love you dad!).

One day during my adult life, it hit me. I finally realized why I had been smoked all those years. It was quite simple…. I LET HIM WIN! That's right, race after race I allowed my dad to leave me in the dust. You see, I never did anything other than talk about how I was definitely going to win the next race. My words were convincing, but while I had a desire to win, I never developed a plan or strategy that would almost guarantee at least one victory for me. I should have prepared to eventually attack a race in such a way that would have challenged my dad, showing him that I had come ready to leave *him* in the dust!

WHAT IS GOAL-SETTING?

A goal is simply...

"Anything I work toward and desire to achieve."

Setting goals is very important. The most successful people in the world are those who set goals. Your favorite teacher, writer, athlete and actor all made decisions about what they wanted in life and then worked to become who they are today. That's how goals operate. The great thing is that goals can be large or small. So whether it's getting your first job or sailing around the world, what matters most is that you do your best to work toward your goals.

List two famous people and someone you personally know who attained success:

1._____

2._____

3._____

If you do a little research on the people you listed above, chances are you will find that they would have never been successful if they had not set personal goals.

At this point you may be thinking, "Sure, goal-setting helped them but what can it really do for me?" The rewards are endless but there are 7 key benefits you should remember...

Goal-setting can:

1. Boost your self-esteem.
2. Improve self-control.
3. Crush procrastination.
4. Ease stress.
5. Improve leadership qualities.
6. Help you stay focused.
7. Develop sense of direction.

Goal Tip #1

"A positive attitude leads to great opportunities."

– Alicia Hadley

What is a positive attitude? Write the definition below.

_____

_____

_____

_____

Why do you think a positive attitude will lead to great opportunities?

_____

_____

_____

_____

"If you have a positive attitude and constantly strive to give your best effort, eventually you will overcome your immediate problems and find you are ready for greater challenges."

— Pat Riley
Former player and coach,
National Basketball Association (NBA)

"If you don't like something, change it. If you can't change it, change your attitude."

— Maya Angelou
Famous American author and poet

Find quotes that encourage you to have a positive attitude. Write them below.

_____

_____

_____

_____

_____

_____

Ask a family member or friend about a time when a positive attitude helped them accomplish a goal. Ask them to suggest things you can do to stay positive. Write their story in the section below.

_____

_____

_____

_____

_____

_____

_____

_____

_____

_____

_____

_____

HOW TO SET GOALS

Now that you understand what goal-setting is and why it's important, you may be wondering how to get started. There are a few simple steps you can follow, and after a bit of practice you'll know them like the back of your hand:

<u>Step 1:</u> *Make a "Wish List" of things you would like to accomplish*

SO MANY THINGS TO CHOOSE FROM!

Have you ever gone to the store and forgotten why you were there? I have. One day I had an urge to bake a homemade cake but realized I was lacking a few ingredients such as milk, eggs, and flour. Naturally, I decided to go to the grocery store to get them. On the way there I received at least two phone calls and when I walked into the store they were having a ridiculous sale—I was in grocery paradise! I grabbed a basket and started shopping. In a matter of minutes my basket was full so I got a cart and continued shopping. Before I knew it, I was at the register with over fifty dollars worth of stuff. Worst of all, I forgot to get milk, eggs, and flour. After putting the groceries in the car, I went back into the store and spent more time and more money buying the ingredients I needed.

During my grocery store ordeal, I made one huge mistake that cost me about forty extra dollars and forty-five more minutes than I had planned. The mistake...I didn't make a grocery list. Now think of your life as a huge grocery store full of possible distractions, unexpected surprises and so many things from which to choose. Clearly, your life needs something similar to a grocery list—something I call a "wish list." A wish list consists of a few things you think you would like to accomplish. It serves as a reminder of potential goals especially when you begin to feel overwhelmed or you have a lot on your mind. You can list anything from having a better relationship with your parents to getting your first cell phone, car or job.

Here's an important thing to remember; without a wish list you'll have a bunch of ideas scattered throughout your brain, making it easy to forget some things. When you write your ideas on paper they become clearer and you won't have as much to remember. Therefore, your brain can relax.

Try It! Go ahead and make a three-item wish list below:

<u>My Wish List</u>

1._____

2._____

3._____

Goal Tip #2

"Avoid distractions." – Alicia Hadley

What are distractions? Give the definition below.

_____

_____

_____

_____

How can distractions affect the outcome of your goals?

_____

_____

_____

_____

_____

_____

Write about a time when you were distracted while trying to complete a task. What was the end-result?

_____

_____

_____

_____

_____

_____

_____

_____

_____

_____

_____

_____

_____

Ask a family member or friend about a time when they allowed distractions to stop them from reaching a goal. Write their story in the section below. What did they learn and what advice can they give you?

_____

_____

_____

_____

_____

_____

_____

_____

_____

_____

_____

_____

Step 2: *Evaluate My Wish List*

DECISIONS, DECISIONS, DECISIONS

My brother had borrowed a Mongoose BMX bike and luckily for me he had forgotten to lock it up. I had always wanted a BMX bike and this particular one was fully loaded. I convinced myself that I could take the bike for a ride and return it before my brother got home. So I took it and went to the corner store. All of my friends were in amazement; I was "the man."

The excitement had me so caught up, I lost track of time. My brother would be home within fifteen minutes... I would have to take the shortcut through a dark path past deep ditches and a vicious dog. Left with no option, I took the path. Sure enough, disaster struck. The vicious dog began to bark and before I knew it, he was chasing me. My heart was pounding! I began riding the bike over tree limbs, rocks, and through ditches faster than I could blink. When I got home the bike was covered in dirt and full of scratches. To top it off, it had a flat tire.

When my brother found out, I was in deep trouble. I had to do his chores, use my allowance to buy a replacement tire and, of course, I was grounded. Taking the bike had turned out to be a really bad decision.   *— Mike (Alicia's husband)*

We usually believe that our ideas are great. But after acting upon them, we discovered that a few of them weren't so great after all.

When you choose to act on bad ideas you miss out on getting the good things in life. If Mike hadn't taken the bike, he would not have wasted his hard earned money on replacing the flat tire. Rather, he could have used the money to purchase his own bike.

List three choices you made and later realized they really weren't the best decisions:

1.

2.

3.

Would you have acted on those ideas if you had first written them down and looked closely at the possible end-result?

When you made your wish list, you listed things you thought would be great accomplishments. But before you start working to accomplish those goals, make sure they are positive. Positive goals are those which will:

1. Help shape and improve your character
2. Lead you to experience beneficial things
3. Ultimately encourage others

The truth is, a negative action that may take two seconds to complete could actually affect you for the rest of your life. However, positive actions do just the opposite — one smart choice could lead to a lifetime of benefits and rewards.

To be sure you work only toward positive goals you'll need to do a "wish list evaluation." List the positive and negative things about each idea on your list. Once you complete the evaluation you can decide which desires are truly positive goals worth pursuing.

Below are a few questions that can help you complete your evaluation. Fill out this section for each of the items on your wish list:

Possible goal #1_____

Who

Who does this potential goal involve?

_____

_____

_____

Who will it affect?

_____

_____

_____

Who (if anyone) am I trying to please by attaining this goal?

_____

_____

_____

What

What could possibly happen?

_____

_____

_____

Could this distract me from focusing on more important things?

_____

_____

_____

If I complete this goal, what might it reveal about me as a person?

_____

_____

_____

Where

Where might I have to go to attain this goal? Is this location safe?

_____

_____

_____

Does this location cause me to compromise who I am or what is right?

_____

_____

_____

When

Is this the right time in my life to work toward this goal or should I wait until later?

_____

_____

_____

Why

Why is this goal important to me?

_____

_____

_____

How

How might this goal affect me in the long-run?

_____

_____

_____

How will it affect my relationship with those whom I love?

_____

_____

_____

How will this goal make me feel about myself?

_____

_____

_____

Possible goal #2_____

Who

Who does this potential goal involve?

_____

_____

_____

Who will it affect?

_____

_____

_____

Who (if anyone) am I trying to please by attaining this goal?

_____

_____

_____

What

What could possibly happen?

_____

_____

_____

Could this distract me from focusing on more important things?

_____

_____

_____

If I complete this goal, what might it reveal about me as a person?

_____

_____

_____

Where

Where might I have to go to attain this goal? Is this location safe?

_____

_____

_____

Does this location cause me to compromise who I am or what is right?

_____

_____

_____

When

Is this the right time in my life to work toward this goal or should I wait until later?

_____

_____

_____

Why

Why is this goal important to me?

_____

_____

_____

How might this goal affect me in the long-run?

_____

_____

_____

How will it affect my relationship with those whom I love?

_____

_____

_____

How will this goal make me feel about myself?

_____

_____

_____

Possible goal #3_____

Who

Who does this potential goal involve?

_____

_____

_____

Who will it affect?

_____

_____

_____

Who (if anyone) am I trying to please by attaining this goal?

_____

_____

_____

What

What could possibly happen?

_____

_____

_____

Could this distract me from focusing on more important things?

_____

_____

_____

If I complete this goal, what might it reveal about me as a person?

_____

_____

_____

Where

Where might I have to go to attain this goal? Is this location safe?

_____

_____

_____

Does this location cause me to compromise who I am or what is right?

_____

_____

_____

When

Is this the right time in my life to work toward this goal or should I wait until later?

_____

_____

_____

Why

Why is this goal important to me?

_____

_____

_____

How

How might this goal affect me in the long-run?

_____

_____

_____

How will it affect my relationship with those whom I love?

_____

_____

_____

How will this goal make me feel about myself?

_____

_____

_____

Below, make a Wish List Evaluation using the "wish list" you previously created. List the pros and cons of each possible goal. Be honest with yourself as you complete this exercise.

Goal Tip #3

"Avoid negative influences." – Alicia Hadley

What are negative influences?

_____

_____

_____

_____

How can negative influences affect you?

_____

_____

_____

_____

_____

Write about a time when negative influences caused you to make a poor choice. What did you learn from the situation?

_____

_____

_____

_____

_____

_____

_____

_____

_____

_____

_____

Ask a family member or friend about a time when negative influences caused them to make poor choices. Write their story in the section below. What did they learn and what advice can they give you?

_____

_____

_____

_____

_____

_____

_____

_____

_____

_____

<u>Step 3:</u> *Write your goal in your "Simple Book of Goals" journal*

WRITE THE VISION

Use your evaluation to decide on the positive goal(s) you wish to start working on right away. Don't overwhelm yourself. There may be a few that you should start working on later in the year or even a few years from now. If you start a goal too soon or too late, you may not get the results you desire. For example, if you want to make the varsity basketball team, don't wait until the week before tryouts to start preparing. You will need as much time as possible to practice and get in good physical shape even if it's a year or two in advance.

Once you've decided on your goal, write it on a "My Goal" page of your "My Simple Book of Goals" journal (If you haven't had a chance to purchase your copy, use a sheet of paper). Use a seperate page for each goal.

Example: I will work toward_____.

Goal Tip #4

"Learn from your past and focus on your future."

— Alicia Hadley

Why should you learn from your past and focus on your future?

_____

_____

_____

_____

_____

_____

_____

_____

_____

"Focus and repetition develops skill."

— Sean Whitaker
Actor and Entreprenuer

"It comes from saying no to 1,000 things to make sure we don't get on the wrong track or try to do too much. We're always thinking about new markets we could enter, but it's only by saying no that you can concentrate on the things that are really important."

— Steve Jobs (1955-2011)
Co-founder, chairman, and CEO of Apple Inc.

Find a quote that encourages you to stay focused. Write it below.

_____

_____

_____

_____

_____

_____

_____

Ask a family member or friend about a time when staying focused helped them achieve a goal. Write their story in the section below. Ask them to suggest things you can do to remain focused.

_____

_____

_____

_____

_____

_____

_____

_____

_____

_____

_____

_____

Step 4: *Remember how this goal can help you and others*

OH THE BENEFITS!

I sat at the keyboard with my head in my hands and tears streaming down my face. Would I ever be able to listen to a song and play it immediately after? I had been practicing for hours and I still couldn't figure out the chords. I felt like tossing my keyboard out the window and throwing in the towel. My desire was to be able to play by ear but it didn't seem to be working. As I sat there, I reminded myself that if I didn't learn this technique I wouldn't be able to help local churches when they needed a musician. I wouldn't be able to play the melodies to the many songs I loved. Was I willing to accept that? Quite frankly, I wasn't! I lifted my head, dried my tears and continued practicing.

I had many disappointing experiences on my quest to play by ear. There were times when people encouraged me but there were also instances when people laughed, whispered, and actually didn't mind if I failed. During those times, I had to remember how this goal could benefit me and my local community. That boosted my determination to remain focused and not give up. Now I'm the organist and keyboard player at my local church. I've played for several soloists and groups, and have composed my very own songs. — *Alicia*

On the journey toward meeting your goals situations may occur that will make you think you won't succeed. People might say things that hurt, discourage and even anger you. The truth is, not everyone will want to see you accomplish your goal. Even the most successful achievers have been hurt and discouraged at some point. But they didn't allow disappointments to cause them to give up and neither should you. The best remedy for discouragement is encouragement. However, there are instances when it seems that encouragement is nowhere to be found. That's when you'll need to encourage yourself.

After completing the "My Goal" section of your goal page go ahead and fill out "How this goal can help me and others." This is one of the most important exercises in your journal. It's the section you will look back on to encourage yourself. You should get a burst of energy when you remind yourself of how much this goal means to you and how it can benefit others — whether it's teaching you patience or putting extra money in your pocket; whatever way it will help, write it down.

Goal Tip #5

"Grab hold of determination and don't let go!"

– Alicia Hadley

What is determination? Write the definition below.

_____

_____

_____

_____

_____

Why must you have determination?

_____

_____

_____

_____

_____

"Determination determines
the success of your destiny."

— April Marcell
Film writer, director and actress

"Those who are blessed with the most talent
don't necessarily outperform everyone else.
It's the people with follow-through who
excel."

— Mary Kay Ash (1918-2001)
Founder of Mary Kay Cosmetics, Inc.

Find a quote that encourages you to have
determination. Write it below.

_____

_____

_____

_____

_____

Ask a family member or friend about a time when determination has helped them achieve a goal. Write their story in the section below.

_____

_____

_____

_____

_____

_____

_____

_____

_____

_____

_____

_____

Step 5: *Information and skills I need to achieve my goal*

FIRST THINGS FIRST

Dressed in a full North Face suit, I arrived at the ski resort excited and ready to take on the slopes. There was one problem — I had never gone skiing! My friend assured me I would be fine and insisted that skiing wasn't as hard as it looked.

While standing at the window to pay for my skiing trip, I was given the option to take a ski lesson with trained instructors. I decided to opt out and just rent my equipment. I put on my ski boots, picked up my skis and headed to the slopes. My friend and his father were both giving me bits of instruction on how to maneuver but while they attempted to instruct, I was busy snapping my boots into the skis. I didn't wait for them to show me any techniques. As soon as I was locked in, I went sliding down the slope. I hadn't been prepared to move and had no clue how to stop! Faster and faster down the hill I went and before I knew it, I was at the bottom — laid out in the snow.

The goal of the trip was to have fun. Unfortunately, because I refused lessons and didn't take time to gather information about the skills needed to ski, most of my day was spent screaming, falling and trying to figure out how to stop.

— *Simone (Alicia's Sister)*

Understanding what's needed to complete a goal is extremely important. Take time to learn the facts about what you wish to accomplish so that you don't have to repeat your efforts. In fact, for some goals, there may not be another opportunity to achieve them.

Maybe your goal is to score at least 95 percent on your next science assignment. The very first thing you must find out is what you need to know and what you need to do. If you simply start the assignment without having the details, you're bound to miss key steps that will aid in your success.

Think about three things you have attempted to do without first finding out about the requirements and skills needed to do them. What was the outcome of each? How could you have been more successful by knowing what was required?

1._____

_____

_____

_____

_____

2._____

_____

_____

_____

_____

3._____

_____

_____

_____

_____

Goal Tip #6

"Patience leads to success." – Alicia Hadley

What is patience? Write the definition below.

_____

_____

_____

_____

_____

How can patience lead to success?

_____

_____

_____

_____

_____

"When you have a dream that you can't let go of, trust your instincts and pursue it. But remember: Real dreams take work, they take patience, and sometimes they require you to dig down very deep. Be sure you're willing to do that."

— Harvey Mackay
Famous businessman and author

"Patience is a growing pain of self-improvement."

— Michael Hadley
Architect and illustrator

Find another quote about patience. Write it below.

_____

_____

_____

_____

_____

Ask a family member or friend about a time when patience helped them achieve a goal. Write their story in the section below. Ask them to suggest things you can do to be patient.

_____

_____

_____

_____

_____

_____

_____

_____

_____

_____

_____

_____

WHAT LIES AHEAD?

The Crucible would be the next school play and the auditions were rapidly approaching. I had to quickly decide if I had the guts to try out and if I did, would I have the discipline to be dedicated to the drama team? I was already on the basketball team, taking advanced placement and honors classes, a writer for the school newspaper, a member of the national honors society and a musician at my church. If the drama team was to be added to my list of responsibilities, I would need to make sure my priorities were kept in order. I thought about the challenges that could come along with being in the drama club and ways to make them easier. Adding an extra activity to my life would mean less leisure time, extra time given to rehearsals and more hours dedicated to studying.

After much consideration, I decided to audition and was awarded a part in the play. Happily, I was able to maintain honors status, continued acting in other drama productions and eventually became a member of the International Thespian Society. I was able to overcome the challenges of adding the drama club to my list of activities because I prepared myself to do so. *– Alicia*

When working toward success there will be challenges—obstacles that make it difficult to reach your goal. Identifying challenges that might lie ahead can better prepare you to face them head on and possibly avoid a few.

What might be difficult about meeting your current goal? What problems may be caused by people, places, and things around you?

Fill out the "Challenges I might face while trying to achieve my goal" section of your goal page. Be sure to list the challenges and what you can do to overcome them. If more space is needed, use one of the "Goal Notes" pages in the back of your "My Simple Book of Goals" journal.

Goal Tip #7

"Self-discipline makes a
rocky road much easier to travel."

— Alicia Hadley

What is self-discipline? Write the definition below.

_____

_____

_____

_____

_____

How can self-discipline make life easier for you?

_____

_____

_____

_____

_____

"Discipline is the bridge
between goals and accomplishment."

-Jim Rohn (1930-2009)
American entrepreneur, author and speaker

"Discipline yourself, and others won't need to."

-John Wooden (1910-2010)
Former basketball player and coach

Find one more quote about self-discipline. Write it below.

_____

_____

_____

_____

_____

Ask a family member or friend how they have used self-discipline to achieve a goal. Write their story in the section below.

_____

_____

_____

_____

_____

_____

_____

_____

_____

_____

_____

_____

Goal Tip #8

"Avoid procrastination." – Alicia Hadley

What is procrastination? Write the definition below.

_____

_____

_____

_____

_____

How can procrastination affect the outcome of your goals?

_____

_____

_____

_____

_____

Write about a time when you procrastinated. What was the end result?

_____

_____

_____

_____

_____

_____

_____

_____

_____

_____

_____

_____

Ask a family member or friend about a time when they procrastinated. Write their story in the section below. What did they learn and what advice can they give to you?

_____

_____

_____

_____

_____

_____

_____

_____

_____

_____

_____

_____

THE MORE, THE BETTER

The weather was perfect for a late night crabbing adventure. A friend of mine had found out about a popular spot called Point Lookout to catch those famous Maryland blue crabs. I asked my husband, Mike, if he felt up to the trip. He replied, "sure." So we packed the car full of crabbing gear and headed for the pier. As we drove, all I could think about was the taste of juicy crab meat smothered in melted butter — those crabs were mine!

When we got to the pier, we could see the crabs swimming through the water. However, the pier was extremely high and the crabs were moving rather fast. We grabbed our long rod nets and began dropping them over the pier, trying to dip the crabs out of the water. Sadly, my friend and I were struggling. Leaning over the pier was wearing us out and the crabs seemed to be slipping straight through our nets. We were taking too long to reel them in. Bunches of crabs were getting away by drifting closer to the bottom as soon as our poles hit the water. I couldn't believe it, we weren't catching any crabs.

Mike, on the other hand, appeared to be having a much easier time catching them. He had formed a technique that seemed to be working. He was already catching crabs and was yelling for us to come help him pull them from the net. My friend and I needed to quickly come up with a strategy that would work for us. Mike was the tallest and fastest in the group, so we decided to ask him to be the one to catch the crabs. My friend and I pulled out flash lights to help him see deeper into the water to prevent the crabs from getting away. When Mike snatched those succulent crustaceans out of the water, we would be ready with our utility gloves to swiftly pull them from the net.

Our plan worked great. We caught a bunch of crabs and as Mike was pulling them from the water, he was sharing his technique with us. Funny thing...Mike isn't really fond of crabs; he went along just because we asked! – *Alicia*

No matter how old you get, never be afraid to ask for help! Most likely, there are others who have accomplished the same or similar type of goal you want to reach. They may be willing to be your mentor or coach throughout the process. These people may include friends, family and other professionals. Ask questions such as:

1. How long did it take?
2. Where can I find more information?
3. Are there specific skills that will help?
4. What are some of the challenges?
5. What are the advantages and disadvantages of meeting that goal?

Go ahead and complete the "Others who can help me achieve this goal" section of your goal page. Choose those who are familiar with your goal or knowledgeable about aspects of what you are trying to do.

Goal Tip #9

"When you run into resistance
don't give up, be persistent."

— Alicia Hadley

What does persistent mean? Write the definition
below.

_____

_____

_____

_____

_____

Why do you need to be persistent to achieve your
goals?

_____

_____

_____

_____

_____

"Persistence beats resistance." – *Unknown*

"Remember that guy that gave up? Neither does anyone else." – *Unknown*

Find a quote that encourages you to stay focused. Write it below.

_____

_____

_____

_____

_____

Ask a family member or friend about a time when being persistent helped them achieve a goal. Write their story in the section below.

_____

_____

_____

_____

_____

_____

_____

_____

_____

_____

_____

_____

A TIME FOR EVERYTHING

In the opening story "I Let Him Win,"I never set a date by which I wanted to achieve my goal. I kept procrastinating because I thought I had all the time in the world to beat my dad. Thankfully this wasn't a real serious goal.

Planning to achieve your goal in an allocated amount of time will make it seem attainable. You'll be able to:

1. Clearly decide how long each step should take to meeting your goal.
2. Notice if/when you are running behind schedule.
3. Track significant progress.

Think about some things you said you want to do but didn't set a date or timeframe for completion. List them below. Did you ever get started with these goals? If so, how long did it take to accomplish each; did it take longer than it should have?

_____   _____

_____   _____

Now, complete the "I plan to achieve my goal by" section of your goal page. Be realistic and give yourself enough time to complete your goal.

Step 9: *Get up and Goal!*

Now that you know the steps to setting and achieving goals, what are you waiting for?

"Don't just sit there...Get up and Goal!"

Download free "Action Plan" worksheets from www.GetUpandGoal.com

Made in the USA
San Bernardino, CA
22 February 2018